Updated
Second Edition

Kid's Box

T0384692

**Workbook 3**
with Online Resources

American English

**Caroline Nixon & Michael Tomlinson**

**Cambridge University Press**
www.cambridge.org/elt

**Cambridge Assessment English**
www.cambridgeenglish.org

Information on this title: www.cambridge.org/9781316627181

First published 2008
Second edition 2015
Updated second edition 2017

20  19  18

Printed in the Netherlands by Wilco BV

*A catalog record for this publication is available from the British Library*

ISBN 978-1-316-62718-1 Workbook with Online Resources 3
ISBN 978-1-316-62753-2 Student's Book 3
ISBN 978-1-316-62702-0 Teacher's Book 3
ISBN 978-1-316-62725-9 Class Audio CDs 3
ISBN 978-1-316-62735-8 Teacher's Resource Book with Online Audio 3
ISBN 978-1-316-62580-4 Flashcards 3 (pack of 109)
ISBN 978-1-316-62789-1 Interactive DVD with Teacher's Booklet 3 (PAL/NTSC)
ISBN 978-1-316-63017-4 Posters 3
ISBN 978-1-316-62710-5 Presentation Plus 3

Additional resources for this publication at www.cambridge.org/elt/kidsboxamericanenglish

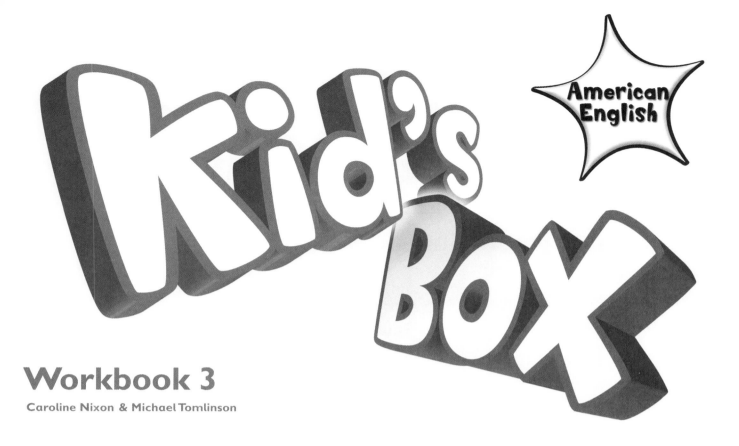

# Kid's Box

American English

## Workbook 3

Caroline Nixon & Michael Tomlinson

| | | |
|---|---|---|
| ⭐ **Hello!** | 4 | |
| **1 Family matters** | 10 | |
| Art – Portraits | 16 | |
| **2 Home sweet home** | 18 | |
| Geography – Homes | 24 | |
| ⭐ **Review 1 and 2** | 26 | |
| **3 A day in the life** | 28 | |
| Science – The heart | 34 | |
| **4 In the city** | 36 | |
| Math – Counting money | 42 | |
| ⭐ **Review 3 and 4** | 44 | |
| **5 Stay healthy** | 46 | |
| Science – A healthy body | 52 | |
| **6 A day in the country** | 54 | |
| Science – Plants | 60 | |

| | | |
|---|---|---|
| ⭐ **Review 5 and 6** | 62 | |
| **7 World of animals** | 64 | |
| Geography – Animal habitats | 70 | |
| **8 Weather report** | 72 | |
| Music – Instruments | 78 | |
| ⭐ **Review 7 and 8** | 80 | |
| **Values 1 & 2** Give and share | 82 | |
| **Values 3 & 4** Love your city | 83 | |
| **Values 5 & 6** Fair play | 84 | |
| **Values 7 & 8** Help the world | 85 | |
| Grammar reference | 86 | |
| Language Portfolio | 89 | |

# Hello!

**1** **Read and complete the sentences.**

reading   ~~name's~~   I'm   nine   sister   comic book

Hello. My name's Suzy Star. I'm five. I have a dog. Her name is Dotty.

**a** Hello. My _name's_ Sally Star. I'm _____ . I have a brother and a _____ .

**b** Hi. _____ Scott Star. I'm eight. I like _____ comic books. This is my favorite _____ .

**2** **Now draw and write about you.**

Hi. My name's _____ .
I'm _____ .
I have a _____ .
_____ name's
_____ .
I like _____ .
This is my favorite
_____ .

**3** **Look and color.**

twenty – gray          eighteen – red          fifteen – green
ten – brown            nineteen – blue         sixteen – purple
fourteen – white       twelve – black          seventeen – orange
thirteen – yellow      eleven – pink

**4** **04 CD1** **Listen and write.**

  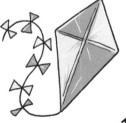   

1  14 kites               5  _____
2  _____    6  _____
3  _____    7  _____
4  _____    8  _____

**5** Match and write.

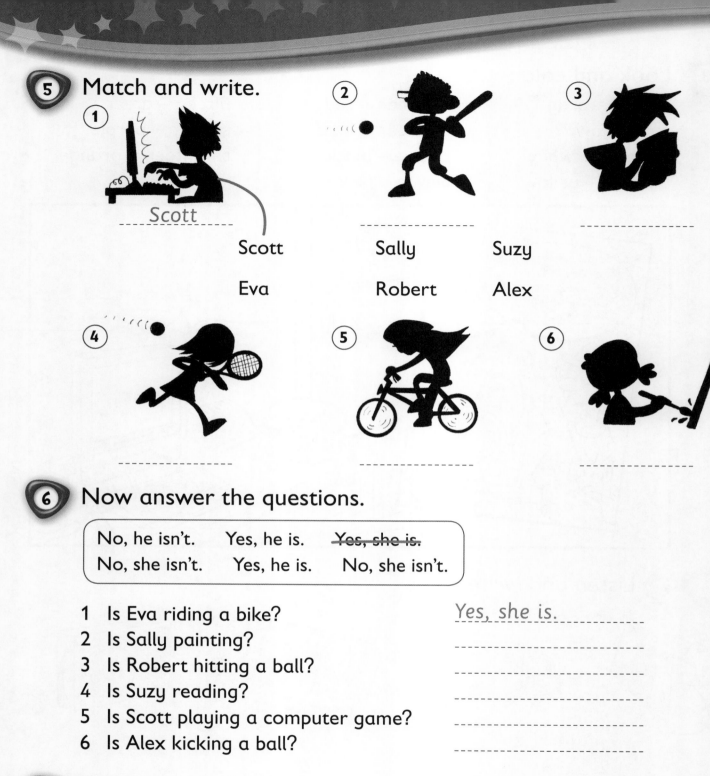

1  Scott

Scott      Sally      Suzy

Eva      Robert      Alex

2  _____

3  _____

4  _____

5  _____

6  _____

**6** Now answer the questions.

| No, he isn't. | Yes, he is. | ~~Yes, she is.~~ |
| No, she isn't. | Yes, he is. | No, she isn't. |

1  Is Eva riding a bike?          Yes, she is.
2  Is Sally painting?             _____
3  Is Robert hitting a ball?      _____
4  Is Suzy reading?              _____
5  Is Scott playing a computer game?  _____
6  Is Alex kicking a ball?        _____

**7** Read and match.

1  Is Lily reading?            a  No, he's drinking.
2  Where's the kite?          b  No, I have a brother.
3  Do you have a sister?      c  She's eating ice cream.
4  Is Jim eating?             d  It's under the bed.
5  What's Daisy eating?       e  Yes. She loves books.

**8** **Read, write, and color.**

Jane, Fred, Vicky, Paul, Stacey, Mary, and Jim are in the park now. Stacey's riding a black bike. Fred's flying a big orange kite. Mary's playing soccer with a small brown dog. The dog's getting the purple ball. Jim's sitting with a fat gray dog. Vicky likes dogs. She's taking pictures with a green camera. Paul's playing field hockey with his cousin, Jane. She's wearing a new yellow T-shirt and old blue jeans.

Stacey

**9** **Look at the picture. Correct the sentences.**

1   Paul's flying a kite.
    No. Fred's flying a kite.

2   Mary has a camera.

3   Jim's playing field hockey.

4   Vicky has a bike.

5   Fred and Stacey have dogs.

6   Jane's getting the ball.

**10** **09** **CD1** Match the rhyming words. Listen, check, and say.

| | | | |
|---|---|---|---|
| 1 red | __e__ | a) | drink |
| 2 sock | _____ | b) | bike |
| 3 door | _____ | c) | white |
| 4 pink | _____ | d) | my |
| 5 like | _____ | e) | head |
| 6 blue | _____ | f) | gray |
| 7 kite | _____ | g) | clock |
| 8 train | _____ | h) | floor |
| 9 fly | _____ | i) | you |
| 10 say | _____ | j) | plane |

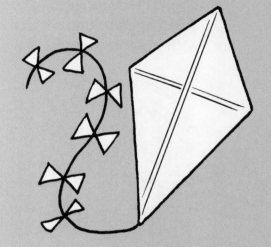

**11** Read and complete the chart.

I have two good friends. Their names are Peter and Daisy. Peter can ride a bike, but he can't swim. He can play the piano, and he can play badminton. Daisy can ride a bike, swim, and play the piano. She can't play badminton.

| Name | Peter | Daisy |
|---|---|---|
| Ride a bike | | ✓ |
| Swim | ✗ | |
| Play the piano | | |
| Play badminton | | |

Now write about your friends.

_My friends_ _____
_____
_____
_____

**12** **(11)** Listen and connect.

CD1

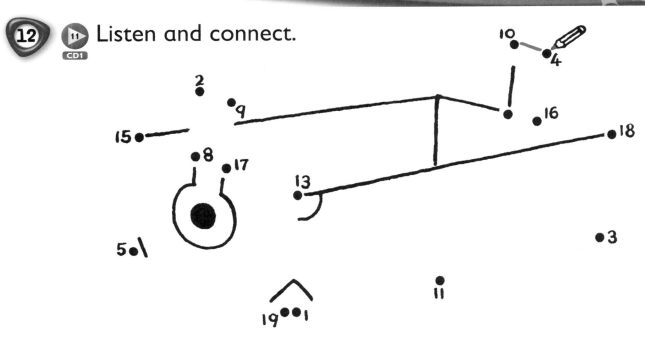

What's this? _____

**13** Complete and answer.

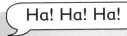

1 What's your favorite comic book called?

_____

2 What's your favorite toy?

_____

3 What's your favorite sport?

_____

4 What's your favorite color?

_____

5 What's your favorite animal?

_____

6 What's your favorite _____?

_____

Ha! Ha! Ha!

You have five apples in one hand and eight apples in the other hand. What do you have?

JOKE BOX

Big hands.

# 1 Family matters

**1** 🔊13 CD1 Listen and match.

a b c d e f

**2** Now complete the sentences.

> son  daughter  parents  granddaughters
> aunt  ~~grandparents~~  uncle  grandson

1 The people on the bus are Sally's _grandparents_ .
2 Grandma Star's _____ is on the bike.
3 The girls in the boat are Grandpa Star's _____ .
4 The woman in the helicopter is Grandma Star's _____ .
5 The boy on the bike is Mr. Star's _____ .
6 Suzy's _____ is in the truck.
7 The people in the plane are Sally's _____ .
8 Scott's _____ is in the helicopter.

**3** Read the sentences. Who is speaking?

**1** Uncle Fred is our uncle.

**2** Scott is our grandson.

**3** Grandma and Grandpa Star are our grandparents.

**4** Suzy and Sally are our granddaughters.

**5** Aunt May is our aunt.

**6** Grandma and Grandpa Star are our parents.

**4** Read and complete the sentences.

The Star family is doing different things. Suzy's in the living room. She's drawing a picture of her Uncle Fred. He's sleeping on the couch. Scott's in the yard. He's playing tennis with his Aunt May. She loves playing tennis with him because he's very good at sports. Sally has a new camera, and she's taking a picture of her grandparents in the dining room. The children's parents are in the kitchen. They're making dinner.

1 The Star _family_ is doing different things.
2 Suzy's drawing a picture of her _____ .
3 Uncle Fred's _____ on the couch.
4 Scott and his _____ are in the yard.
5 Scott's very _____ at sports.
6 Sally's taking a picture of her _____ .
7 Grandma and Grandpa Star are in the _____ .
8 The children's _____ are in the kitchen.

**5** Read and circle the best answer.

1 Suzy: Do you enjoy shopping?
  Uncle Fred: a) I have a new T-shirt.
                  b) No, I don't.

2 Suzy: Does Grandma like painting?
  Uncle Fred: a) Yes, I do.
                  b) Yes, she loves painting.

3 Suzy: Does Sally want to be a doctor?
  Uncle Fred: a) Yes, she does.
                  b) Yes, she can.

4 Suzy: Do you enjoy playing tennis?
  Uncle Fred: a) Yes, he does.
                  b) No, Aunt May enjoys playing tennis

5 Suzy: Does Dotty like taking baths?
  Uncle Fred: a) No, she doesn't.
                  b) She loves swimming.

6 Suzy: Do you wear your a helmet on your bi
  Uncle Fred: a) Yes, I do.
                  b) Scott's riding his bike.

**6** Look and match the sentences.

1 Uncle Fred has a bike.
2 Grandpa has a camera.
3 Scott has a ball.
4 Mr. Star has a guitar.
5 Sally has a book.
6 Grandma has some eggs.

a She wants to read it.
b He wants to take a picture.
c She wants to make a cake.
d He wants to play it.
e He wants to ride it.
f He wants to play basketball.

**7** Find and write the words.

| b | e | a | r | d | l | m | n | a | s | t | i |
|---|---|---|---|---|---|---|---|---|---|---|---|
| q | u | i | e | t | o | p | a | r | b | a | n |
| e | g | i | h | o | s | c | u | r | l | y | h |
| d | u | k | e | s | s | a | g | e | s | r | k |
| f | u | n | n | y | a | s | h | e | m | u | l |
| v | a | r | t | y | o | m | t | i | k | y | c |
| e | g | h | f | p | o | a | y | s | o | v | s |
| b | x | r | a | t | b | r | g | a | l | t | d |
| m | c | h | i | l | b | t | a | r | d | c | a |
| s | a | s | r | s | t | r | a | i | g | h | t |

1  tasmr  _____smart_____
2  haynugt  _____
3  utqei  _____
4  rebad  _____
5  unyfn  _____
6  lucyr  _____
7  gittshra  _____
8  aifr  _____

**8** Ask and answer. Complete the chart.

Do you enjoy singing?

Yes, I do. ✓

No, I don't. ✗

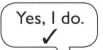
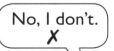

| Do you enjoy ... | ♫ singing? | ⚃ playing games? | 📖 reading? | 🖌 painting? |
|---|---|---|---|---|
|  |  |  |  |  |
|  |  |  |  |  |

**9** **Listen and say. Circle the word that doesn't belong.**

| | | | |
|---|---|---|---|
| 1 | day | paint | (park) |
| 2 | say | star | name |
| 3 | car | train | plane |
| 4 | play | farm | gray |
| 5 | cake | arm | eight |
| 6 | game | make | p_a_rty |
| 7 | May | take | yard |
| 8 | start | b_a_by | straight |

  **10** **Listen and color and write. There is one example.**

results

Ha! Ha! Ha!

What's a quiet animal called?

JOKE BOX

A shhh-eep

# Do you remember?

 Look and read     Say     Fold the page     Write the words     Correct

 _parents_ _____     parents

 _____     son

 _____     daughters

 _____    aunt

 _____    uncle

 _____    grandparents

 _____    grandson

 _____    granddaughters

 _____    curly

_____    straight

_____    beard

## Can do

I can write "family" words.   

I can describe my friends and family.   

I can say what I want.

**1** Read and write the names.

| 1 | |
|---|---|
| 2 | |
| 3 | Nick |
| 4 | |
| 5 | |
| 6 | |

a Daisy is Tom's daughter. She has straight fair hair.

b Nick has short black hair. He's Tom's son.

c Aunt Clare has curly hair.

d Sally is Daisy and Nick's mom. She has straight fair hair.

e Nick and Daisy's uncle has short gray hair and a beard.

f The man with curly hair is Daisy's father.

g Daisy's standing next to her Uncle Jack.

**2** Circle the one that doesn't belong.

1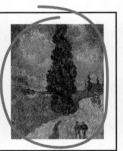

2

3

4

**3** **23** CD1 Listen and color and write. There is one example.

**1** Match. Write the words.

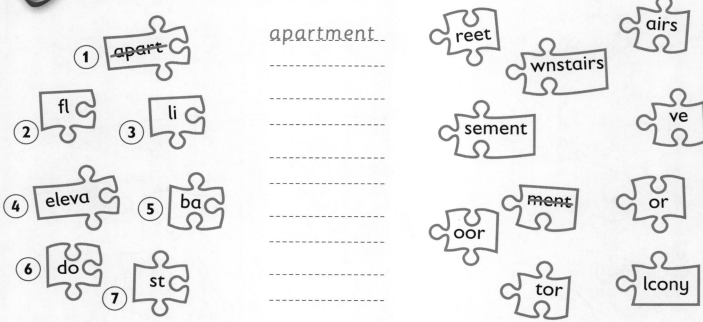

apartment

------------------

------------------

------------------

------------------

------------------

------------------

------------------

**2** Complete the crossword puzzle.

Down ↓    Across →

**3** **Read and complete.**

> downstairs ~~town~~ upstairs floors balcony street

Robert lives in a small (1) _town_ . There are five houses on his

(2) _____ . His house has three (3) _____ . Robert walks

(4) _____ to his bedroom because there isn't an elevator. The living

room and the kitchen are (5) _____ . His house doesn't have a

(6) _____ , but it has a beautiful yard.

**4** **Write about your home. Draw.**

I live in a _____

_____

_____

_____

_____

_____

**5** Read and circle.

1 Eva's (taking) / climbing a lamp upstairs.
2 The men are carrying / going the couch upstairs.
3 My mom's carrying / sitting on the couch.
4 Eva's taking / smiling because she's happy.
5 The boy's climbing / going the tree.
6 The children are smiling / drinking water.
7 Charlie's going / taking up in the elevator.
8 The men are taking / sitting a break.

**6** Read and complete. Match.

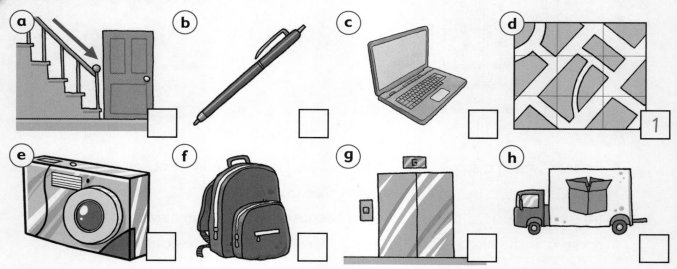

1 We want to find our friend's street. We need a _map_ .
2 He's eighty and can't climb the stairs. He needs to use the _____ .
3 She wants to write her address on the letter. She needs a _____ .
4 You want to carry your books and pencils to school. You need
  a _____ .
5 I want to take a picture of my bedroom. I need a _____ .
6 They want to move to a new house. They need a moving _____ to
  take their beds and other furniture to their new home.
7 He wants to play his new computer game. He needs his _____ .
8 She wants to go to the basement. She needs to walk _____ .

**7** Match the words and numbers.

| 1 | 90 |
|---|---|
| 2 | 18 |
| 3 | 40 |
| 4 | 17 |
| 5 | 50 |
| 6 | 60 |
| 7 | 20 |
| 8 | 13 |

_twenty_    ewttyn

_____    ifytf

_____    etrhinet

_____    txisy

_____    niyten

_____    tihgeeen

_____    ofytr

_____    neevnetes

**8** Read and color.

I live at number 83, and my balcony is gray. The balcony above mine is green. The balcony below mine is blue. The balcony at number 95 is red. The balcony between number 93 and the red one is purple. The balcony next to number 73 is orange. There's a pink balcony above the orange one. The balcony next to the orange one is yellow. The balcony at number 85, above the yellow one, is brown.

**9** **Listen and say. Write the words.**

~~yellow~~   ~~brown~~   house   wind<u>ow</u>   nose   town
down   throw   out   know   coat   clown

**boat**
yellow
_____
_____
_____
_____
_____

**cloud**
brown
_____
_____
_____
_____
_____

 **10** **Read and complete the chart.**

Jack lives in an apartment in a city. His apartment has a balcony, but it doesn't have a yard. He can play in the basement below his apartment.

Mary lives in a very big house in the country. Her house has a yard and a basement, but it doesn't have a balcony.

Stacey lives in a small apartment in a city. Her apartment doesn't have a basement or a yard, but it has a beautiful balcony with a lot of of flowers.

Paul lives in a city. His house doesn't have a balcony or a basement, but it has a small yard with an apple tree.

|  | city | country | apartment | house | yard | balcony | basement |
|---|---|---|---|---|---|---|---|
| Jack |  |  |  |  |  |  |  |
|  |  |  | ✓ |  |  |  |  |
|  |  |  |  |  |  | ✗ |  |
|  |  | ✓ |  |  |  |  |  |

Ha! Ha! Ha!

Doctor, doctor, there are monsters under my bed. What can I do?

JOKE BOX

Sleep on the couch.

# Do you remember?

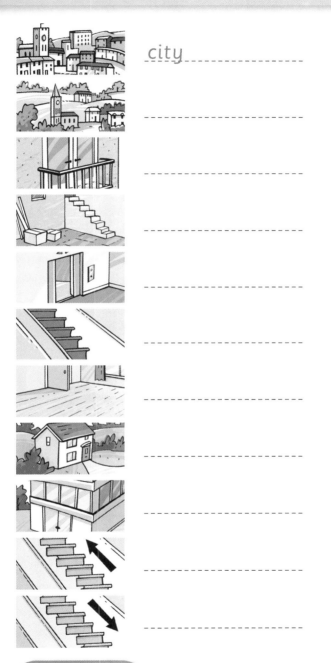

city _____

_____

_____

_____

_____

_____

_____

_____

_____

_____

_____

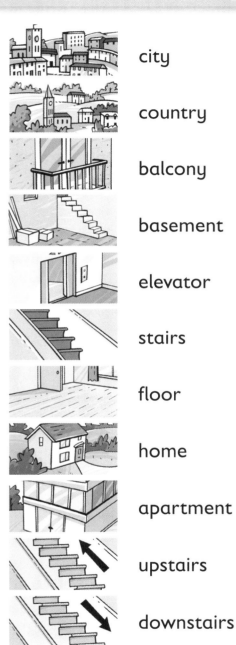

city

country

balcony

basement

elevator

stairs

floor

home

apartment

upstairs

downstairs

## Can do

I can talk about where people live.

I can describe my house.

I can count to 100.

**1** Choose and match. Where do they live?

 Sue   Ben   Lucy   Tom   Anna

**2** Now ask and match.  Where does Sue live?   She lives in a tree house.

 Sue   Ben   Lucy   Tom   Anna

**3** Now complete the sentences.

| castle | house | apartment | ~~tree house~~ | houseboat |

1. Sue lives in a _tree house_ .
2. Ben lives in a _____ .
3. Lucy lives in _____ .
4. Tom lives _____ .
5. Anna _____ .

Read the text and choose the best answer.

Charlie is talking to his friend Lily.

**Example**

| Charlie: | What are you looking at? |
| Lily: | (A) I'm looking at a picture. |
| | B I can't find my book. |
| | C Yes, I am. |

**Questions**

1 Charlie: Is this your house?
  Lily:    A Yes, in an apartment.
           B No, thanks.
           C No, it's that one.

2 Charlie: Do you like living in the country?
  Lily:    A Yes, you do.
           B Yes, I love it.
           C No, I like soccer.

3 Charlie: Do you have a yard?
  Lily:    A Yes, we do.
           B No, we can't.
           C Yes, we aren't.

4 Charlie: Is your aunt wearing a gray jacket?
  Lily:    A No, it's my favorite color.
           B Yes, she is.
           C Yes, it's blue.

5 Charlie: Is there a store next to your house?
  Lily:    A Yes, there's an amusement park.
           B Yes, forty-three.
           C Yes, there is.

6 Charlie: Do you enjoy taking pictures of your family?
  Lily:    A Yes, please.
           B Yes, I like it a lot.
           C No, a banana.

# Review Units  1 and 2

**1**   Listen and write the numbers.

① ② ③ ④ ⑤ ⑥

68

**2** Read and find.

We're looking for the pet thief's uncle.
Can you help us?
He has short straight hair. He isn't fair.
He has a big black beard.
He's wearing a black shirt.
He doesn't have a hat.

①   ②   ③   ④

⑤   ⑥   ⑦   ⑧

**3** Circle the one that doesn't belong.

| | | | |
|---|---|---|---|
| 1 (down) | granddaughter | grandson | parents |
| 2 quiet | smart | balcony | naughty |
| 3 daughter | son | uncle | doctor |
| 4 country | basement | town | city |
| 5 fair | curly | straight | forty |
| 6 song | hair | beard | mustache |
| 7 door | move | window | wall |
| 8 mirror | telephone | supermarket | lamp |
| 9 house | store | home | apartment |
| 10 above | between | behind | listen |

**4** Now complete the crossword puzzle. Write the message.

# 3 A day in the life

**1** Check and order the sentences. What do you do every day?

| | | |
|---|---|---|
| a | I take a shower. | ☐ |
| b | I get up. | ☐ |
| c | I get undressed. | ☐ |
| d | I go to bed. | ☐ |
| e | I have dinner. | ☐ |
| f | I have lunch. | ☐ |
| g | I wake up. | ✓ |
| h | I have breakfast. | ☐ |
| i | I go to school. | ☐ |
| j | I get dressed. | ☐ |

| 1 | g |
|---|---|
| 2 | |
| 3 | |
| 4 | |
| 5 | |
| 6 | |
| 7 | |
| 8 | |
| 9 | |
| 10 | |

**2** Look and read and write.

Example  The door in the big room is _open_____

**Complete the sentences.**

1  The man with the beard is _____ .

2  The _____ with curly hair is getting up.

**Answer the questions.**

3  What is the man with the mustache doing?        _____

4  What is the time on the clock?        _____

**Now write two sentences about the picture.**

5  _____

6  _____

28

**3** Look and match.

a

b

Ten o'clock
Eleven o'clock
Seven o'clock
Six o'clock
Three o'clock
One o'clock

c

d

e

f

**4** Write "before" or "after."

1  I take off my clothes ___before___ I take a shower.
2  I wash my hands _____ I have lunch.
3  I take off my shirt _____ I take off my jacket.
4  I put on my socks _____ I put on my shoes.
5  I go to bed _____ I have dinner.
6  I get dressed _____ I go to school.

Now write two more sentences.

7  _____
8  _____

**5** Talk to your friend.
Is your routine the same or different?

Do you get dressed after breakfast?

Yes, I do.

Different! I get dressed before breakfast.

Do you take a shower before bedtime?

No, I don't.

Same!

**6** **Find and write the words.**

| e | f | n | j | a | m | i | h | f | t |
|---|---|---|---|---|---|---|---|---|---|
| a | m | b | i | s | o | c | p | l | h |
| s | t | u | t | c | n | k | a | o | u |
| s | a | t | u | r | d | a | y | u | r |
| u | a | l | e | b | a | n | k | l | s |
| n | r | g | s | c | y | l | a | w | d |
| d | h | d | d | e | i | h | a | k | a |
| a | y | x | a | f | r | i | d | a | y |
| y | i | d | y | l | s | w | b | a | m |
| w | e | d | n | e | s | d | a | y | a |

S u n d a y

M _ _ _ _ _

T _ _ _ _ _ _ _

W _ _ _ _ _ _ _ _ _

T _ _ _ _ _ _ _

F _ _ _ _ _

S _ _ _ _ _ _ _

**7** **Look, read, and write.**

_____  _____  _____

_____

_____  Monday  _____

1 Peter always plays basketball after school on Mondays.
2 On Tuesdays Jim and Stacey play badminton after school.
3 Jack and Mary do their homework after school on Wednesdays.
4 Daisy has a swimming class on Thursdays. She never watches TV.
5 Mary and Fred watch TV with their mom on Friday evenings.
6 Paul goes shopping with his dad on Saturday mornings.
7 Vicky plays soccer on Sundays. She sometimes scores a goal.

**8** Use the words to make three sentences.

| Clare Vicky Paul Jack Stacey Daisy | sometimes always never | wakes up has dinner watches TV goes to bed takes a shower gets dressed | in the kitchen. at seven o'clock. after dinner. in the evening. in the morning. before breakfast. |

Now play bingo.

| Clare | never | takes a shower | in the kitchen. |
|---|---|---|---|
| | | | |
| | | | |
| | | | |

**9** Write sentences about you.

I wake up at _____ o'clock every day. _____

_____

_____

_____

_____

**10** Write new words. Use the letters from this sentence.

Charlie and Paul never have breakfast at eight o'clock.

1 _score_____   4 _____

2 _____   5 _____

3 _____   6 _____

**11** 🔊 43 CD1  **Listen and say. Circle the word that doesn't belong.**

| | | | |
|---|---|---|---|
| 1 | horse | (book) | st<u>or</u>y |
| 2 | box | short | sport |
| 3 | door | board | down |
| 4 | f<u>or</u>ty | four | old |
| 5 | you | floor | more |
| 6 | small | house | ball |
| 7 | doll | d<u>augh</u>ter | w<u>a</u>ter |

**12** **Read and complete the story.**

On Mondays Paul wakes up at 🕐 (1) _____ . He gets up and always takes a

🚿 (2) _____ . Then he gets dressed and goes to the 🍳 (3) _____ for

breakfast. After breakfast he puts on his 🧥 (4) _____ , and he goes to the bus stop

to catch a 🚌 (5) _____ . He never walks to 🏫 (6) _____ .

At 🕐 (7) _____ Paul comes home and does his homework before dinner.

After dinner he sometimes plays on his 💻 (8) _____ .

He goes to 🛏 (9) _____ at ⏰ (10) _____ .

Ha! Ha! Ha!

Why do you go to bed every night?

Because the bed can't come to you!

JOKE BOX

32

# Do you remember?

 Look and read   Say   Fold the page   Write the words   Correct

 _wake up_  wake up

 -------------------  get up

 -------------------  take a shower

 -------------------  get dressed

 -------------------  catch the bus

 -------------------  do my homework

 -------------------  wash my hands

 -------------------  get undressed

 ------------------- ... go to bed

## Can do

I can talk about my daily routine.

I can say how often I do things.

I can say the days of the week.

33

**1**  Match.

> The heart   blood from the body   oxygen   blood to the lungs   blood to the body

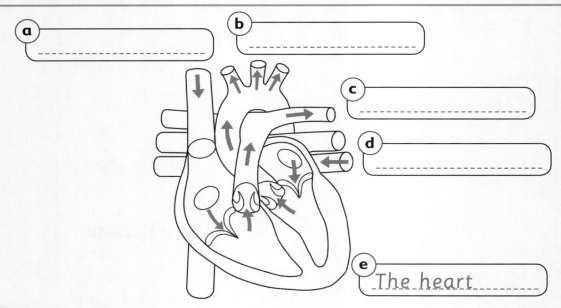

a _____

b _____

c _____

d _____

e The heart_____

**2**  Complete the chart. Write sentences.

| Activity | Is your pulse quick? |
|----------|----------------------|
| Running  | ✓ |
| Smiling  | ✗ |
| Sleeping |  |
| Reading  |  |
| Jumping  |  |
| Dancing  |  |

1  Your pulse is quick when you run.
2  Your pulse isn't quick when you smile
3  Your pulse _____
4  Your pulse _____
5  Your _____
6  _____

**3**  Read. Write "yes" or "no."

1  Your blood is blue.                                        _no_____
2  Your heart moves blood in your body.                       _____
3  Your heartbeat is quick when you exercise.                 _____
4  Your blood sends milk to your heart.                       _____
5  Your heartbeat is slow when you jump.                      _____
6  When you play sports, your body needs more oxygen.         _____

**What food does Lily have in these places?**

Listen and write a letter in each box. There is one example.

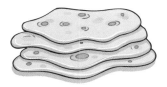 pancakes  H

 banana

 ice cream

 sandwich

 candy

 cake

 A

 B

 C

 D

 E

 F

 G

 H

**1** Sort and write the words.

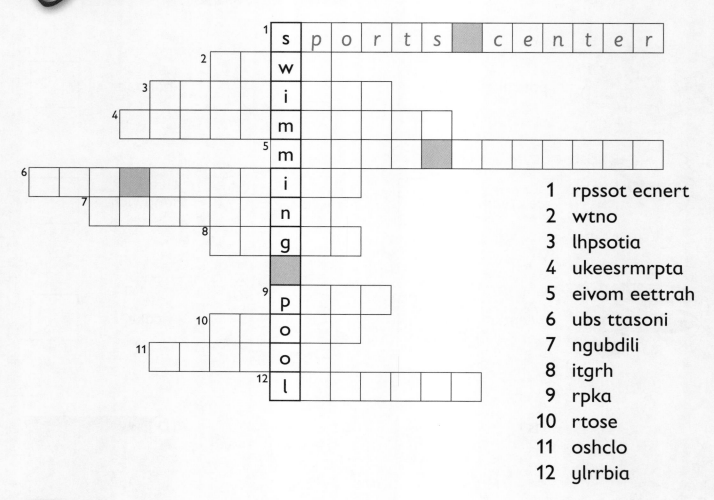

1  rpssot ecnert
2  wtno
3  lhpsotia
4  ukeesrmrpta
5  eivom eettrah
6  ubs ttasoni
7  ngubdili
8  itgrh
9  rpka
10  rtose
11  oshclo
12  ylrrbia

**2** Look at the code. Write the secret message.

| 26 | 25 | 24 | 23 | 22 | 21 | 20 | 19 | 18 | 17 | 16 | 15 | 14 |
|---|---|---|---|---|---|---|---|---|---|---|---|---|
| a | b | c | d | e | f | g | h | i | j | k | l | m |
| 13 | 12 | 11 | 10 | 9 | 8 | 7 | 6 | 5 | 4 | 3 | 2 | 1 |
| n | o | p | q | r | s | t | u | v | w | x | y | z |

T h e r e's / _ / _ _ _ _ _ _ _ _ / _ _ _ _ /
7-19-22-9-22'-8 / 26 / 8-4-18-14-14-18-13-20 / 11-12-12-15 /

_ _ _ _ / _ _ / _ _ _ / _ _ _ _.
13-22-3-7 / 7-12 / 7-19-22 / 25-26-13-16

**3** Look, read, and write. Match.

1 You go there to buy food and drink.          _supermarket_
2 You go there to read books.                   _____
3 You go there to play tennis and volleyball.   _____
4 You go there to get money.                     _____
5 You go there to see movies.                    _____
6 You go there to catch a bus.                   _____
7 You go there to swim, and you wear a swimsuit. _____
8 You go there to buy good fruit and vegetables. _____

**4** Complete the picture. Answer the questions.

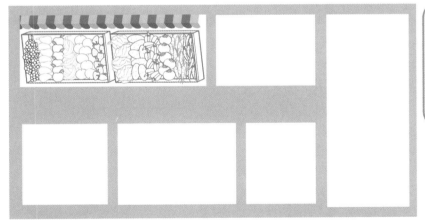

~~market~~    bus station
movie theater
parking lot
sports center     library

1 Where's the market?         _The market is next to the_ _____.
2 Where's the bus station?    _____.
3 Where's the movie theater?  _____.
4 Where's the parking lot?    _____.
5 Where's the sports center?  _____.
6 Where's the library?        _____.

**5** Read and circle the best answer.

1 You must be quiet in a
  a) sports center   b) library   c) park

2 To catch a bus you must go to the
  a) movie theater   b) bus station   c) hospital

3 You must clean
  a) the supermarket   b) the bus station   c) your bedroom

4 To fly your kite you must go to
  a) the supermarket   b) the library   c) the park

5 You must sit down in the
  a) market   b) swimming pool   c) movie theater

6 To see a doctor you must go to a
  a) hospital   b) park   c) market

7 You must take money to a
  a) park   b) supermarket   c) library

8 To see a movie you must go to the
  a) movie theater   b) swimming pool   c) sports center

**6** Read and match.

Suzy must clean her bedroom. She must put the books in the bookcase. She must put her kite on the closet and her T-shirt in the closet. She must put her pencils on the desk next to the computer and her shoes under the bed. She must put her toy box between the bed and the bookcase.

**7**  **Read and check. Listen and check.**

At school we must:

| | |
|---|---|
| answer the teacher's questions | ✓ |
| listen to the teacher | |
| wear pants | |
| run on the playground | |
| come to class with a pencil | |
| eat our lunch in the cafeteria | |
| raise our hands to speak | |
| sit next to our friends in the library | |
| do our homework | |
| drink on the playground | |
| speak English in class | |

**8** **Write. What must you do at home?**

do homework   go to bed   clean bedroom   brush teeth
clean shoes   make bed   put books in bookcase

*I must brush my teeth*

**Listen and say. Circle the words with the "s" sound.**

1 (city)　　2 center　　3 comic book

4 catch　　5 face　　6 computer

7 uncle　　8 balcony　　9 place

10 clean　　11 exciting　　12 dance

**10 Put the words in groups.**

granddaughter　circus　upstairs　wake up
uncle　basement　movie theater　daughter　have lunch
parent　store　floor　get up　hospital　balcony　library
elevator　grandson　catch　play　aunt　café　wash　downstairs

| Actions | Places | Home | Family |
|---------|--------|------|--------|
|  |  |  |  |
| wake up | circus | upstairs | granddaughter |

Ha! Ha! Ha!

Doctor, doctor, I think I need glasses.

JOKE BOX

Yes, you do. This is the library!

40

# Do you remember?

 **Look and read**   **Say**   **Fold the page**   **Write the words**   **Correct**

 circus _____

 circus

 _____

 bus station

 _____

 movie theater

 _____

 library

 _____

 market

 _____

 supermarket

 _____

 sports center

 _____

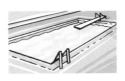 swimming pool

## Can do

I can write "city" words.

I can talk about places in my city.

I can talk about things I must do.

**1** Do the math.

 $24
 $1
 $15
 $60
 $8
 $6

1 Stacey wants a ball and a computer game.   $8 + $24 = $32
2 Lily wants a comic book and a watch.   $1 + $15 = $_____
3 Jack wants a watch and a kite.   $_____ + $_____ = $21
4 Fred wants a camera and a _____.   $_____ + $1 = $_____
5 Jane wants a _____ and a ball.   $_____ + $_____ = $14
6 I want a _____ and a _____.   $_____ + $_____ = $_____

**2**  Look at the menu. Read and answer.

1 Four children are in a café. They have ten dollars. Nick wants a chicken salad. Jill wants some ice cream. Tom wants some chocolate cake, and Pat wants some milk.

How much money do they need?
$6.05 _____

What else can they buy?

_____

2 Now you're in the café. You have six dollars. You'd like egg salad, some carrot cake, and some lemonade.

How much money do you need?

_____

What else can you buy?

_____

### ❀ Menu ❀

| | |
|---|---|
| Fish, rice, and salad | $3.95 |
| Chicken salad | $2.25 |
| Egg salad | $1.75 |
| Burger | $1.65 |
| Apple cake | $1.30 |
| Carrot cake | $1.45 |
| Chocolate cake | $1.60 |
| Ice cream | $1.25 |
| Milk | 95¢ |
| Lemonade | $1.15 |
| Pineapple juice | $1.25 |
| Orange juice | $1.10 |

**3** Read the story. Choose a word from the box. Write the correct word next to numbers 1–5. There is one example.

My name is Jack. I'm ten years old, and I live in a house in the _country_ . Behind my house there's a big **(1)** _____ . I go there with my **(2)** _____ , Bonny. Bonny enjoys going there very much. She loves running and catching a ball. I like going there after school. I play with my friends.

My school is in a big city. I must catch a bus to school, but I can **(3)** _____ to the bus stop. It's next to my house!

I enjoy going to the city on Saturdays, too. I always go shopping with my mom. We go to the big **(4)** _____ between the sports center and the library. We buy our food for the week there.

After shopping I sometimes go to the library to get a good **(5)** _____ to read.

**Example**

| country | walk | dog | ice cream | supermarket |

| book | park | climb | school |

**(6)** Now choose the best name for the story.
Check one box.

Jack's dog    ☐

Jack's week    ☐

Jack's school    ☐

# Review Units 3 and 4

**1** Read and order the words. Make sentences.

| | | | | |
|---|---|---|---|---|
| 1 | play tennis | on | I sometimes | Wednesdays. |
| 2 | 7 o'clock. | wakes up | Tom never | before |
| 3 | on | Mary never | the weekend. | rides her bike |
| 4 | before | dinner. | wash our hands | We always |
| 5 | do their homework | in | the evening. | Jim and Peter never |
| 6 | Sunday mornings. | read | on | They always |

1 _I sometimes play tennis on Wednesdays._

2 _____

3 _____

4 _____

5 _____

6 _____

**2** Find the words.

movietheateralwayswimarketownneverreadaughterobotellibraryestationeedinner

Now answer the questions.

How many town words are there? _____

What are they? _____

_____

44

## 3 Circle the one that doesn't belong.

1  car     truck     bus     (feet)

2  lunch     shower     breakfast     dinner

3  afternoon     school     teacher     homework

4  Monday     Saturday     bedtime     Friday

5  always     sneakers     sometimes     never

6  library     movie theater     stairs     market

7  brother     teacher     mother     father

8  children     between     behind     above

9  evening     morning     afternoon     Tuesday

10  never     get up     wash     wake up

## 4 Now complete the crossword puzzle. Write the message.

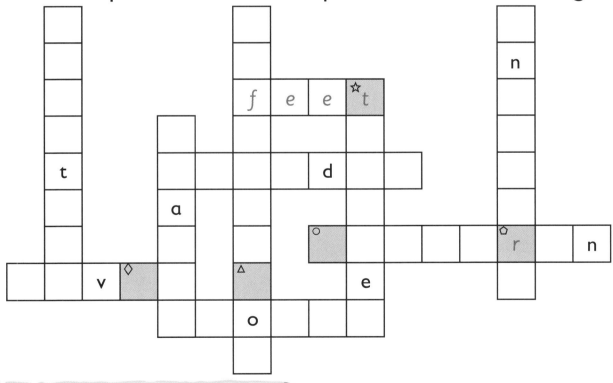

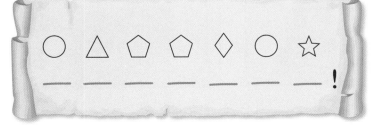

———  ———  ———  ———  ———  ———  ———  !

# 5 Stay healthy

## 1 Write the words.

| ear | tooth | back | stomach | ~~head~~ | foot | hair |
|-----|-------|------|---------|----------|------|------|
| eye | mouth | shoulder | nose | hand | leg | arm |

1 *head*
2 _____
3 _____
4 _____
5 _____
6 _____
7 _____

8 _____
9 _____
10 _____
11 _____
12 _____
13 _____
14 _____

## 2 Complete the sentences.

| temperature | toothache | stomachache | ~~cold~~ | headache | cough |
|-------------|-----------|-------------|----------|----------|-------|

I have a _____*cold*_____ .

I have a _____ .

I have a _____ .

I have a _____ .

I have a _____ .

I have a _____ .

**3** Read and circle.

1 My eye / leg / ear hurts. I can't read.

2 My toe / back / tooth hurts. I can't eat.

3 My shoulder / foot / finger hurts. I can't kick the ball.

4 My leg / ear / eye hurts. I can't ride my bike.

5 My nose / mouth / arm hurts. I can't play tennis.

6 My foot / hand / knee hurts. I can't catch the ball.

**4** Look at Activity 3. Write.

What's the matter?

My eye hurts.
I can't read.

What's the matter?

My _____
I can't _____

What's _____ matter?

_____
_____

What's the _____?

_____
_____

What's _____ _____?

_____
_____

_____ _____ _____?

_____
_____

**5** 🔊 **Listen and write the number.**

a

b

c

d

e
1

f

**6** **Write "must" or "must not."**

Soccer practice on Tuesday.

**Class rules**

1 We _must not_ eat in class.
2 We _____ drink in class.
3 We _____ listen to our teacher.
4 We _____ do our homework.
5 We _____ speak English.
6 We _____ write on the table.
7 We _____ help our teacher.
8 We _____ hit our friends.

Play Field hockey!

Lunch

Fish and salad.

Catch the school bus at 8 o'clock.

**7** Look and match.

(1)

(2)

(3)

(4)

(5)

(6) Aaachoo!

You must not:

play computer games

go swimming

eat a burger and fries

listen to music

eat cake, cookies, or chocolate

pick up a big bag

**8** Now write sentences.

1 _When you have a stomachache, you must not eat a burger and fries._

2 _____

3 _____

4 _____

5 _____

6 _____

**9**  **Match the rhyming words. Listen, check, and say.**

| | | | | | | | |
|---|---|---|---|---|---|---|---|
| 1 | see | _d_ | a) door | 7 | fly | _____ | g) do |
| 2 | hurt | _____ | b) cough | 8 | can't | _____ | h) buy |
| 3 | cake | _____ | c) fun | 9 | two | _____ | i) hair |
| 4 | off | _____ | d) key | 10 | time | _____ | j) aunt |
| 5 | one | _____ | e) shirt | 11 | late | _____ | k) climb |
| 6 | four | _____ | f) ache | 12 | wear | _____ | l) straight |

**10** **Read and order the words. Make sentences.**

| | | | | |
|---|---|---|---|---|
| 1 | go swimming | Fred can't | is sick. | because he |
| 2 | sleep | must not | in class. | We |
| 3 | has a temperature. | stay in bed | Vicky must | because she |
| 4 | Daisy must not | has a backache. | because she | carry big bags |
| 5 | must | We | with toothpaste. | brush our teeth |
| 6 | with | the matter | What's | Jack? |

1 _Fred can't go swimming because he is sick._
2 _____
3 _____
4 _____
5 _____
6 _____

Ha! Ha! Ha!

**What kind of dog always has a temperature?**

JOKE BOX

A hot dog.

# Do you remember?

 Look and read   Say   Fold the page   Write the words   Correct

 *a cold* ------------

 a cold

 ------------

 a cough

 ------------

 a temperature

 ------------

 a headache

 ------------

 a stomachache

 ------------

 a toothache

 ------------

 an earache

 ------------

 a backache

## Can do

I can write "parts of the body" words.

I can say what's wrong with me.

I can talk about things I must not do.

**1** Find the "healthy" words.

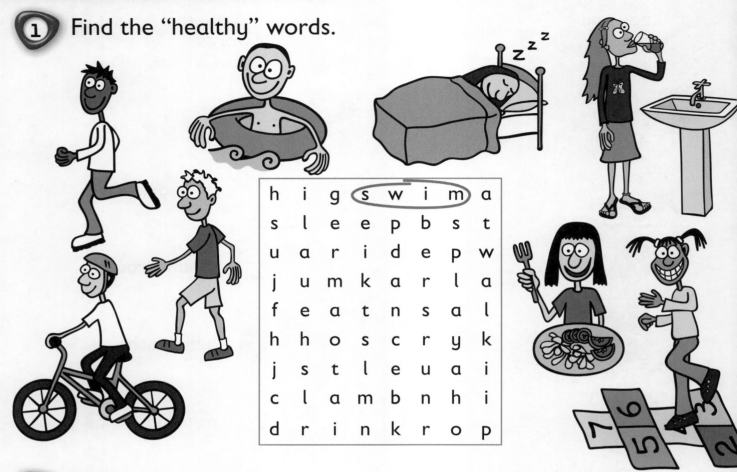

| | | | | | | | | |
|---|---|---|---|---|---|---|---|---|
| h | i | g | s | w | i | m | a |
| s | l | e | e | p | b | s | t |
| u | a | r | i | d | e | p | w |
| j | u | m | k | a | r | l | a |
| f | e | a | t | n | s | a | l |
| h | h | o | s | c | r | y | k |
| j | s | t | l | e | u | a | i |
| c | l | a | m | b | n | h | i |
| d | r | i | n | k | r | o | p |

**2** Check (✓) or put an ✗ in the boxes. Is it healthy?

**3** Look and read and write.

**Examples**

There are eight ____chairs____ in the room.

What is the baby doing? ___sleeping___

**Questions**
**Complete the sentences.**

1 The boy has a cold and he is wearing a striped _____

2 In the poster, the park is between a library and a _____

**Answer the questions.**

3 What's the man with the black shoes doing? _____

4 Where are the books? _____

**Now write two sentences about the picture.**

5 _____

6 _____

# 6 A day in the country

**1** Sort and write the words.

1 virer *river*
2 ldfei _____
3 soreft _____

4 nplta _____
5 keal _____

6 flae _____
7 sgasr _____

**2** Read the text. Write "yes" or "no."

The Stars enjoy going to the country for picnics. Sally loves looking at plants and their leaves and drawing them in her notebook. Suzy enjoys playing on the grass. Scott loves swimming in the lake and walking in the forest with his map. Grandpa loves fishing in the river and sleeping on a towel or a blanket after lunch.

Dotty loves running in the fields, but she must always stay with the family because sometimes there are other animals.

1 The Stars don't like going to the country for picnics.     *no*
2 Sally loves looking at bikes.     _____
3 Sally draws plants and their leaves.     _____
4 Suzy enjoys playing on the blanket.     _____
5 Scott loves swimming in the lake.     _____
6 Grandpa loves swimming in the river.     _____
7 Dotty loves sleeping in the fields.     _____
8 Sometimes there are animals in the fields.     _____

**3** Ask your friend. Complete the questionnaire.

# Free time questionnaire

1 Do you enjoy going to the country?
yes ☐  no ☐

2 How often do you go on picnics?
every weekend ☐  sometimes ☐  never ☐

3 What do you sit on when you're in the country?
the grass ☐  a towel ☐  a blanket ☐

4 How often do you go fishing?
every weekend ☐  sometimes ☐  never ☐

5 Do you enjoy walking in the forest?
yes ☐  no ☐

6 Do you like climbing trees?
yes ☐  no ☐

7 How often do you go swimming in rivers or lakes?
every weekend ☐  sometimes ☐  never ☐

8 Do you like looking at plants and flowers?
yes ☐  no ☐

**4** Look at Activity 3. Write about your free time.

In my free time I enjoy going
I            go on picnics.
I like

**5** Find the pairs and number the pictures.

1

| 1 | cold | 6 | thin |
|---|------|---|------|
| 2 | loud | 7 | hot |
| 3 | strong | 8 | thirsty |
| 4 | hungry | 9 | quiet |
| 5 | fat | 10 | weak |

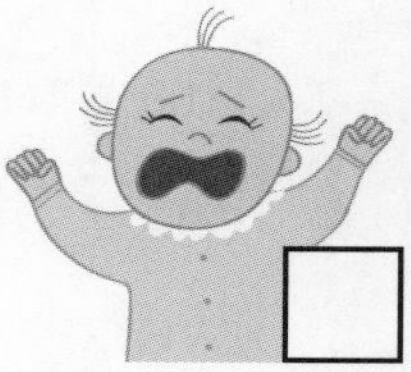

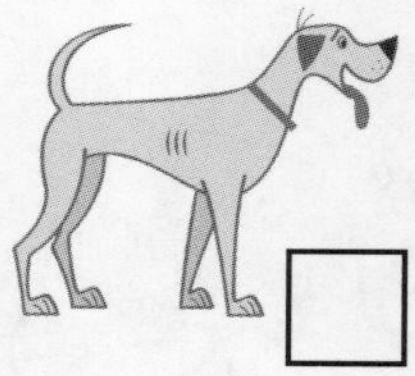

**6** Read and write the sentences.

Should I get a blanket? [ 1 ]    Should I make lunch? [ ]    Should I get a chair? [ ]

Should I get you an ice-cream cone? [ ]    Should I get you a drink? [ ]

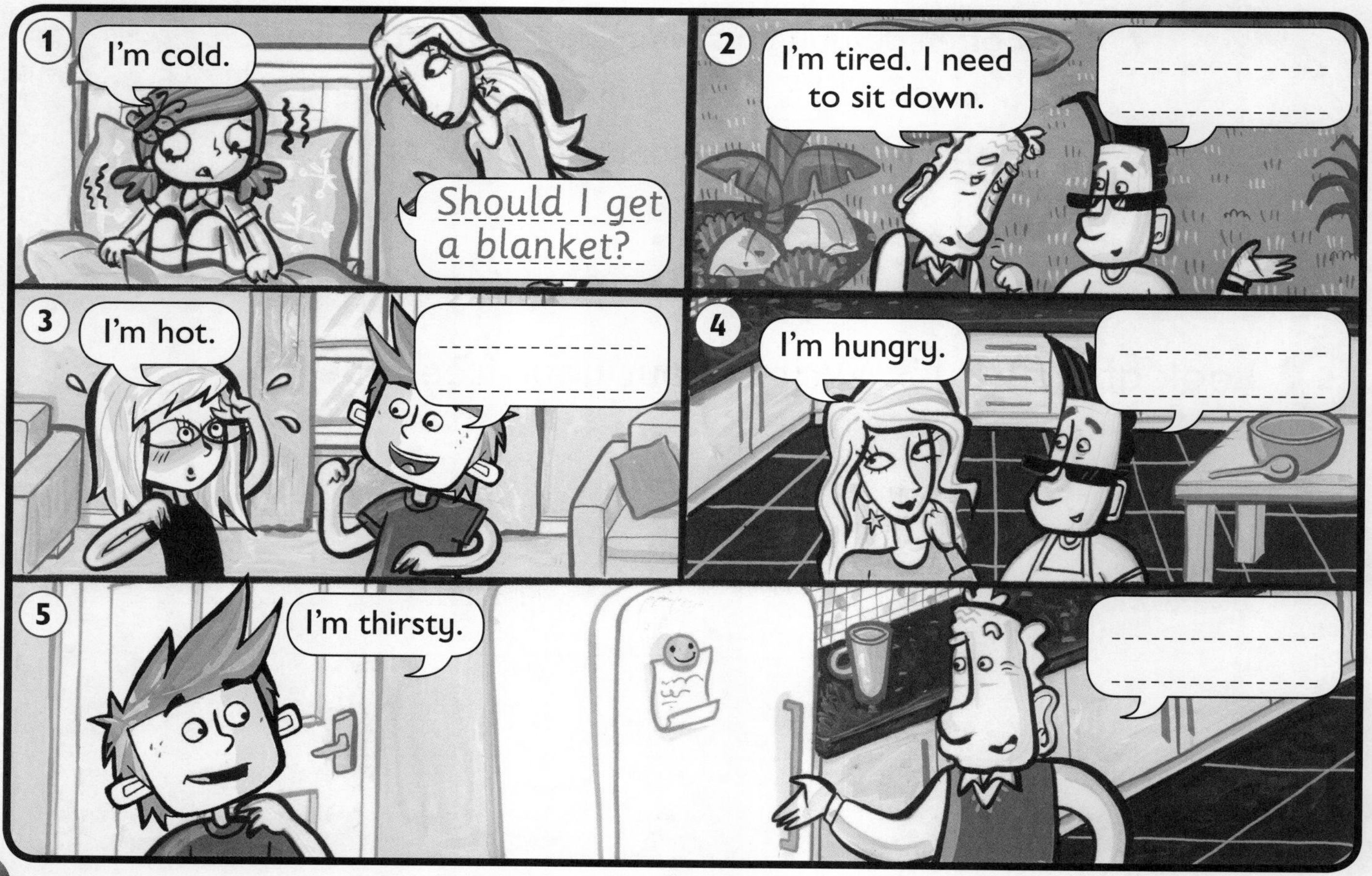

1  I'm cold.    Should I get a blanket?

2  I'm tired. I need to sit down.    --------------

3  I'm hot.    --------------

4  I'm hungry.    --------------

5  I'm thirsty.    --------------

**7** Put the words in groups.

good       hungry       thin       strong

~~weak~~

| Words to describe people | Words to describe people and places |
|---|---|
| weak | |

bad

hot

fat

thirsty       quiet       cold       loud

**8** Look and read. Correct the sentences.

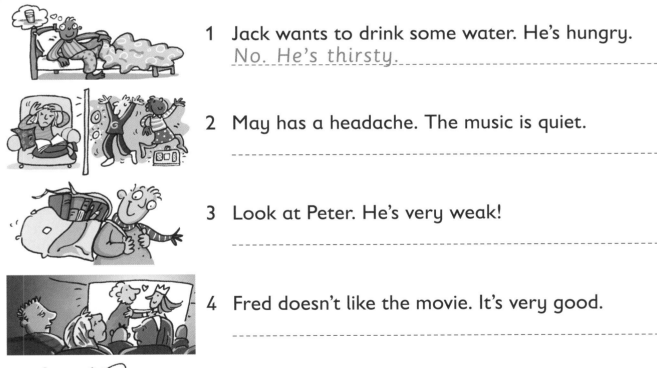

1 Jack wants to drink some water. He's hungry.
   No. He's thirsty.

2 May has a headache. The music is quiet.

3 Look at Peter. He's very weak!

4 Fred doesn't like the movie. It's very good.

5 Anna needs to eat. She's thirsty.

6 Jim's wearing a jacket and a hat. It's hot today.

**Listen and say. Circle the word that doesn't belong.**

| | | | | |
|---|---|---|---|---|
| 1 | green | (red) | eat | please |
| 2 | cheese | street | sleep | head |
| 3 | leaf | bread | see | team |
| 4 | h<u>ea</u>lthy | dream | weak | sheep |
| 5 | she | we | help | three |
| 6 | r<u>ea</u>dy | need | tree | p<u>e</u>ople |
| 7 | meat | teeth | clean | friend |

  **Listen, color, and write.**

 Ha! Ha! Ha!

**What can you see in the center of a field?**

The letter "e"!

**58**

# Do you remember?

 Look and read   Say   Fold the page   Write the words   Correct

 forest ---------------      forest

 -----------------      plant

 -----------------      leaf

 -----------------      grass

 -----------------      field

 -----------------      lake

 -----------------      hungry

 -----------------      thirsty

 -----------------      cold

## Can do

I can talk about the country.   

I can talk about things I like doing.   

I can make suggestions.

**1** Write the words.

| lettuce   roots   orange tree   carrots   sunflower   ~~leaves~~   fruit   seeds |

**a**
leaves

**b**
_____

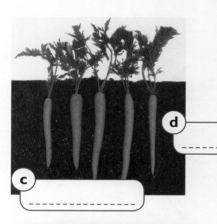

**d**
_____

**c**
_____

**e**
_____

**f**
_____

**h**
_____

**g**
_____

**2** Which part do we eat? Complete the chart.

| orange   ~~potato~~   carrot   apple   spinach |
| pea   lettuce   sunflower   pear   cabbage |

| Roots | Seeds | Leaves | Fruit |
|-------|-------|--------|-------|
| potato |  |  |  |
|  |  |  |  |
|  |  |  |  |

60

**3** Look and read. Choose the correct words and write them on the lines.
There is one example.

a leaf

a plant

a field

a lake

a tree

a forest

a picnic

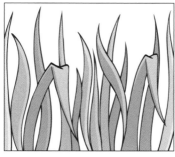

grass

## Example

This is usually green. You must water it every day.          *a plant*

## Questions

1  This is on the ground. It's green, and sheep eat it.          ----------------------

2  We sometimes eat this in the country.          ----------------------

3  This is the name for a lot of trees in the country.          ----------------------

4  Apples grow on this.          ----------------------

5  You can see horses and cows here in the country.          ----------------------

6  This is part of a plant or a tree. It's often small and green.          ----------------------

# Review Units  5 and 6

**1** Choose your adventure.

Come to | Treetop Mountain
Coolwater Lake | . Here you can go | swimming
climbing | , so

remember to bring | strong shoes
a swimsuit | . You can see | beautiful birds
fantastic fish | , and

you can walk | in dark forests
on clean beaches | . It's hot and sunny, so you must bring

| a hat
water | . You must not | catch animals
fish | here.

Remember to bring your | map
bag | and have fun!

**2** Look at Activity 1. Write.

My adventure

Come to ...

Here you can go ...

_____

_____

_____

_____

_____

_____

## 3 Circle the one that doesn't belong.

| | | | | |
|---|---|---|---|---|
| 1 | temperature | cough | cold | ~~shoulder~~ |
| 2 | hungry | sleep | eat | play |
| 3 | eyes | hurts | ears | arms |
| 4 | stomach | headache | backache | toothache |
| 5 | lake | river | ocean | field |
| 6 | leaf | loud | good | bad |
| 7 | run | swim | climb | fat |
| 8 | grass | plant | picnic | flower |
| 9 | hungry | grass | thirsty | tired |
| 10 | loud | weak | quiet | blanket |

## 4 Now complete the crossword puzzle. Write the message.

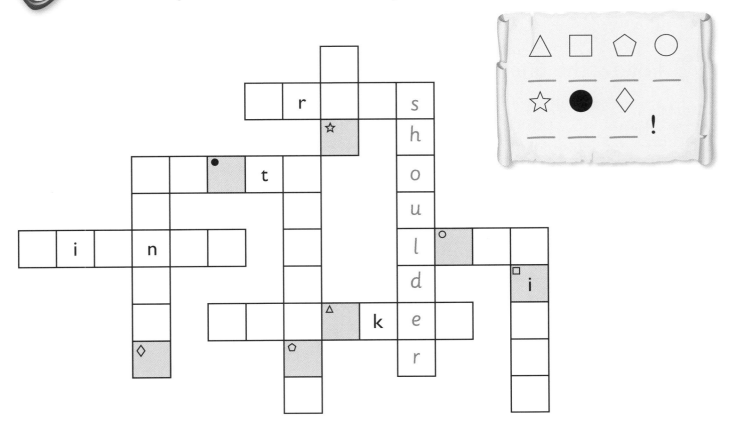

**1** Put these animals in alphabetical order.

1  bat _____
2  _____
3  _____

4  _____
5  _____
6  _____

7  _____
8  _____
9  _____

**2** Follow the animals. Answer.

Start →

| bear | panda | kangaroo | lion | library | funny |
|------|-------|----------|------|---------|-------|
| hospital | clean | strong | whale | hungry | fish |
| thirsty | dolphin | elephant | giraffe | smart | tiger |
| long | crocodile | movie theater | huge | mouse | bat |
| naughty | shark | monkey | parrot | hippo | market |

Finish

How many animals are there? _____

There are four city words. What are they? _____

There are nine adjectives. What are they? _____

_____

**3** Look at the animals. Read and correct.

1 This animal has two legs and a lot of hair on its feet. It eats chocolate and sleeps a lot. It's a big dog.

This animal has four legs

2 This big green animal lives in Africa. It has two short, weak legs and two short, fat arms. It can fly. It carries its picnic in a bag next to its head.

3 This big purple or yellow animal can fly, but it isn't a bird. It eats ice cream and small cookies. It dances in the day and wakes up and sings at night.

**4** Write about your favorite wild animal.

My favorite wild animal is

**5** **Read and circle.**

1 Kangaroos are smaller / (bigger) than bats.
2 Crocodiles are shorter / longer than lizards.
3 Parrots are quieter / louder than mice.
4 Horses are quicker / slower than cows.
5 Giraffes are shorter / taller than hippos.
6 Bears are stronger / weaker than monkeys.

**6** **Look at the picture. Read and write "yes" or "no."**

1 The bear's cleaner than the monkey.
_yes_____

2 The bear's sadder than the monkey.
_____

3 The bear's hungrier than the monkey.
_____

4 The monkey's hotter than the bear.
_____

5 The monkey's dirtier than the bear.
_____

6 The bear's happier than the monkey.
_____

**7** Read and match. Write the words on the chart.

| | | | | |
|---|---|---|---|
| 1 | strong | j | a | cleaner |
| 2 | hungry | ☐ | b | easier |
| 3 | good | ☐ | c | dirtier |
| 4 | dirty | ☐ | d | weaker |
| 5 | clean | ☐ | e | hungrier |
| 6 | bad | ☐ | f | thinner |
| 7 | weak | ☐ | g | quieter |
| 8 | fat | ☐ | h | worse |
| 9 | easy | ☐ | i | hotter |
| 10 | thin | ☐ | j | stronger |
| 11 | quiet | ☐ | k | better |
| 12 | hot | ☐ | l | fatter |

| long**er** | big**ger** |
|---|---|
| stronger | |
| | |
| | |

| happ**ier** | different! |
|---|---|
| | |
| | |
| | |

**8** Color and write.

1  The gray lion's younger than the white one. _____

2  _____

3  _____

4  _____

5  _____

6  _____

**08 CD3 Listen and say. Complete the words.**

1 a dol_ph_in    2 a _____rog    3 a _____otograph    4 a _____armer

5 an ele_____ant    6 a _____ield    7 _____ruit    8 a _____one

**10 Sort and write the words.**

1  tberet      b_etter_____
2  geibgr      b_____
3  tedirir     d_____
4  ireeas      e_____
5  rodle       o_____
6  rtqiuee     q_____
7  lsalmre     s_____
8  gonsterr    s_____
9  sower       w_____
10 tefart      f_____

**11 Now find the words.**

| r | d | u | j | m | o | l | d | e | r |
|---|---|---|---|---|---|---|---|---|---|
| b | i | g | g | e | r | r | t | g | e |
| m | r | x | w | p | m | j | i | q | a |
| s | t | r | o | n | g | e | r | u | s |
| e | i | e | r | t | q | f | a | i | i |
| b | e | i | s | p | w | p | v | e | e |
| x | r | o | e | u | m | i | a | t | r |
| s | m | a | l | l | e | r | b | e | o |
| s | j | q | f | a | t | t | e | r | n |
| b | e | t | t | e | r | a | g | b | s |

Ha! Ha! Ha!

**What do lions call smaller animals?**

Food!

# Do you remember?

 Look and read   Say   Fold the page   Write the words   Correct

 _panda_ _____    panda

 _____    kangaroo

 _____    dolphin

 _____    whale

 _____    shark

 _____    penguin

 _____    lion

 _____    bear

 parrot

## Can do

I can talk about wild animals.

I can talk about where animals live and what they eat.

I can compare things.

**1** Sort and write the words.

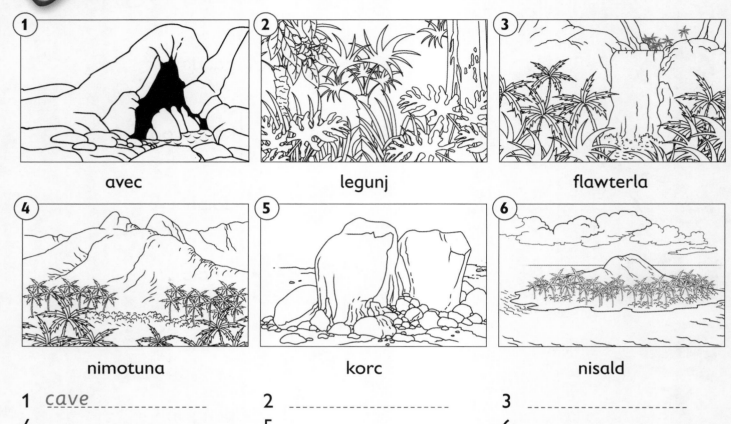

1 avec

2 legunj

3 flawterla

4 nimotuna

5 korc

6 nisald

1 cave_____  2 _____  3 _____

4 _____  5 _____  6 _____

**2** Listen. Write the words.

monkey  bear  bat  dolphin  snake  parrot  lizard  shark

a monkey_____

b _____

c _____

d _____

e _____

f _____

g _____

h _____

**3** **12** **CD3** **Listen and write. There is one example.**

**Charlie's school project**

| | | |
|---|---|---|
| | When? | _Wednesday_ |
| 1 | How many animals? | ------------------------------ |
| 2 | Which kind of animals? | ------------------------------ |
| 3 | Charlie's favorite animal: | ------------------------------ |
| 4 | Favorite animal's food: | ------------------------------ |
| 5 | Name of project: | ------------------------------ |

# 8 Weather report

**1** Look and read and write.

a cloud

the sun

~~the wind~~

a rainbow

the snow

the rain

1  It's strong.                              *the wind*
2  It's hot and yellow.                      ----------------
3  It's wet.                                 ----------------
4  It's cold and white.                      ----------------
5  It's beautiful and has many colors!       ----------------
6  It's white, gray, or black.               ----------------

**2** Read and circle the correct answer.

1  It's hot and (sunny) / snowing.
2  It's wet and sunny. There's a beautiful windy / (rainbow.)
3  It's very gray and cloudy / sunny today.
4  I can make a snowman. There's a lot of snow / sun.
5  We can't go out to play. It's wet and gray. It's raining / sunny.
6  Let's go to the beach. It's a beautiful sunny / windy day.
7  It's snowing / raining in the jungle.
8  It's a beautiful day. It's dry / wet and sunny. Let's have a picnic.
9  It's wet and cloudy. It's raining / rainbow.
10  It's snowing / rainbow in the mountains.

**3** 🔊 **15** **Listen and draw the weather.**

  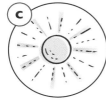   

**4** **Now complete the sentences.**

1 In the mountains _it's windy._
2 In the city _____
3 In the forest _____
4 At the lake _____
5 In the country _____
6 At the beach _____

**5** Read and complete the sentences.

> wasn't ~~was~~ sweater were was scarf great

Last weekend, Eva (1) __was__ in the mountains with her family.
They (2) _____ on vacation. There (3) _____ a lot of snow.
It was (4) _____ ! Eva (5) _____ cold because she was in a hat
and (6) _____ , and she had a (7) _____ under her coat.

**6** Look at the code. Write the secret message.

| 26 | 25 | 24 | 23 | 22 | 21 | 20 | 19 | 18 | 17 | 16 | 15 | 14 |
|----|----|----|----|----|----|----|----|----|----|----|----|----|
| a | b | c | d | e | f | g | h | i | j | k | l | m |
| 13 | 12 | 11 | 10 | 9 | 8 | 7 | 6 | 5 | 4 | 3 | 2 | 1 |
| n | o | p | q | r | s | t | u | v | w | x | y | z |

W e /_ _ _ _ / _ _ / _ _ _ / _ _ _ _ _ _ _ / _ _ _ _/_ _ _ _ .
4-22 / 4-22-9-22 / 18-13 / 7-19-22 / 17-6-13-20-15-22 / 15-26-8-7 / 4-22-22-16 .

_ _/_ _ _ _ ' _/_ _ _ _/_ _ _ _/_ _ _ _ _ _/, _ _ _ /
18-7 / 4-26-8-13- ' 7 / 4-22-7 / 26-13-23 / 4-18-13-23-2 , 26-13-23 /

_ _ /_ _ _ _ _ _ ' _/_ _ _ _ _ / . _ _/_ _ _ _/, _ _ _ _ .
4-22 / 4-22-9-22-13- ' 7 / 24-12-15-23 / . 18-7 / 4-26-8 / 21-6-13 .

**7** Ask and answer. Choose words from the box.

| at home | at a friend's house | at school | at the movie theater | in bed |

at the library in the park at the store at the sports center

Where were you on Monday afternoon?

I was at the sports center.

|  | Me | Friend 1 | Friend 2 | Friend 3 | Friend 4 |
|---|---|---|---|---|---|
| Monday afternoon |  |  |  |  |  |
| Tuesday evening |  |  |  |  |  |
| Wednesday night |  |  |  |  |  |
| Thursday morning |  |  |  |  |  |
| Friday evening |  |  |  |  |  |

**8** Write about your weekend.

On Saturday morning I was

On Sunday morning

**9** **Listen and say. Complete the sentences.**

| whale | ~~What's~~ | windy | wearing | waterfall |

1 _What's_ the weather like? It's wet and _____ .

3 Where were you on Friday? I was at the _____ .

2 Why are you _____ a sweater? Because it's cold today.

4 What's your favorite wild animal? It's a _____ .

**10** **Choose the words. Draw the picture.**

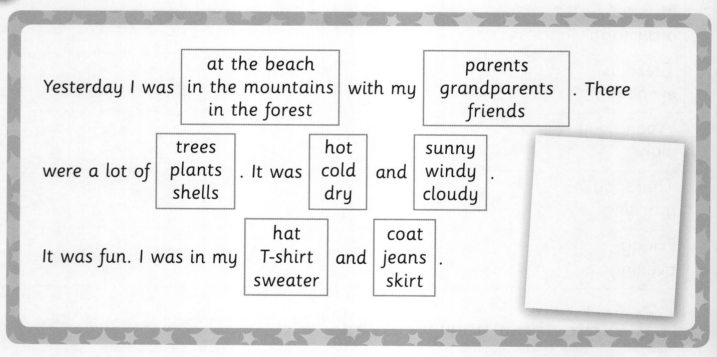

Yesterday I was | at the beach / in the mountains / in the forest | with my | parents / grandparents / friends | . There were a lot of | trees / plants / shells | . It was | hot / cold / dry | and | sunny / windy / cloudy | .

It was fun. I was in my | hat / T-shirt / sweater | and | coat / jeans / skirt | .

 Ha! Ha! Ha!

**Which is quicker, hot or cold?**

 JOKE BOX

Hot, because you can catch a cold.

# Do you remember?

 Look and read     Say     Fold the page     Write the words     Correct

 _cloud_ _____       cloud

 _____       sun

 _____       rain

 _____       wind

 _____       snow

 _____       rainbow

 _____       hot

 _____       wet

## Can do

I can talk about the weather.    

I can write "weather" words.    

I can talk about where I was yesterday.    

77

**1** Match.

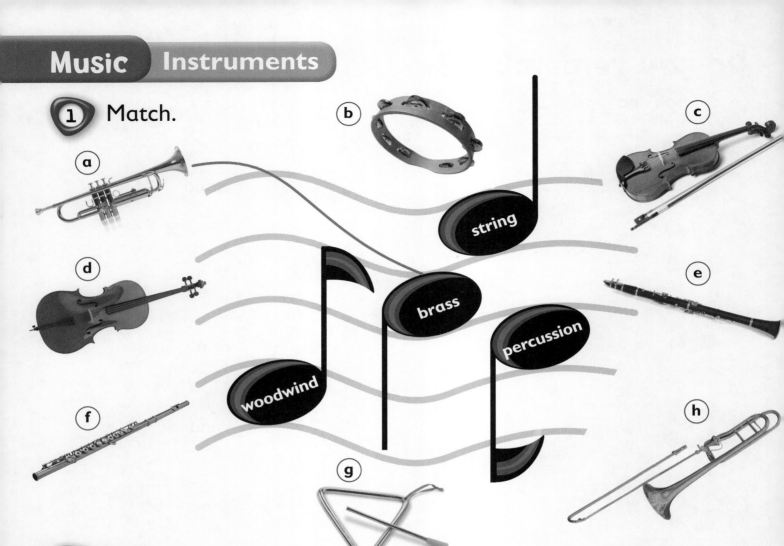

a ·
b ·
c ·
d ·
e ·
f ·
g ·
h ·

string
brass
percussion
woodwind

**2** Music quiz.

1 An orchestra is
   a) a musical instrument.   b) a big group of musicians.   c) a piece of music.
2 You hit this kind of instrument to make music.
   a) percussion   b) brass   c) woodwind
3 You play woodwind and brass instruments with your
   a) hands and feet.   b) mouth and feet.   c) mouth and hands.
4 How many families of musical instruments does an orchestra have?
   a) 2   b) 3   c) 4
5 A violin is a
   a) woodwind instrument.   b) string instrument.   c) percussion instrument.
6 People who play musical instruments are called
   a) musicians.   b) musicals.   c) families.

**3** **Read the text. Choose the right words and write them on the lines.**

The weather

Example    The weather _changes_____ at different times of year.

1    When there _____ a lot of gray clouds in the sky,

it often rains. When it's raining and sunny, we can sometimes

2    see _____ rainbow. Rainbows are very beautiful

3    _____ they have a lot of colors. Sometimes you

can see two rainbows in the sky.  When it's hot and sunny,

4    _____ people enjoy going to the beach. They go

swimming and have picnics. But in some countries, it gets very, very

5    hot, and people _____ go outside in the afternoon.

In the mountains, it often snows when it's very cold. There is always

snow on the top of some very big mountains.

| Example | change | changes | changing |
|---------|--------|---------|----------|
| 1 | are | is | am |
| 2 | a | the | an |
| 3 | but | or | because |
| 4 | all | every | many |
| 5 | aren't | don't | haven't |

# Review Units 1 and 8

**1** Read, color, and draw.

Squawk

Look at the animals. On the island there are two bears. The bear with the fatter stomach is brown, and the other bear is gray. Can you see the snakes?
The green snake is longer than the yellow one. In the cave there are two bats. The black bat is smaller than the gray bat. There are two birds in the trees. They're parrots. The red parrot is louder than the yellow parrot.

There are two whales in the ocean. The blue whale is bigger than the black and white whale.

There's a boat close to the island. Draw a man in the boat. He's wearing a coat and a scarf. He's very hot. The man is looking at the fruit in the trees on the island. He's hungry.

**2** **Circle the one that doesn't belong.**

| | | | | |
|---|---|---|---|---|
| 1 | penguin | shark | (panda) | whale |
| 2 | kangaroo | rainbow | shark | lion |
| 3 | wind | snow | rain | beach |
| 4 | dry | scarf | sweater | coat |
| 5 | parrot | bat | bear | bird |
| 6 | wet | hat | cold | dry |
| 7 | sunny | dirty | windy | cloudy |
| 8 | weaker | better | weather | hotter |
| 9 | easier | worse | thinner | teacher |
| 10 | raining | country | mountains | beach |

**3** **Now complete the crossword puzzle. Write the message.**

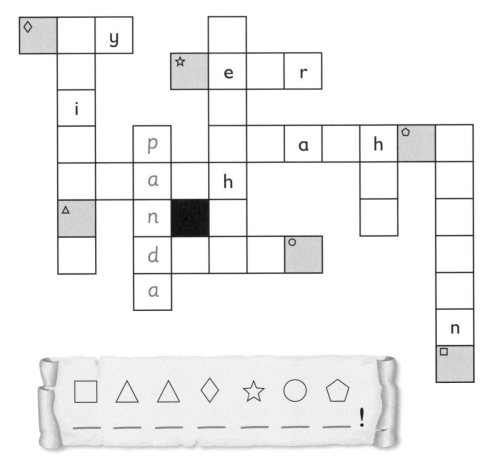

**1**   **Listen and number.**

**2** **Read and choose.**

**1** You have some toys. You don't want them. Do you:

  a) Ask for some more new toys?

  b) Throw them out the window?

  c) Give them to the hospital?

**2** Your friend wants to play with your game. Do you:

  a) Share your game?    b) Say "no"?    c) Break the game?

**3** Your good clothes are too small for you. Do you:

  a) Give them to your young cousins, brothers, or sisters?

  b) Put them in the trash can?

  c) Clean your shoes with them?

**4** You have two of the same toy. Do you:

  a) Play with the two toys?

  b) Put one in a box under the bed and never play with it?

  c) Share with a friend?

**1** Read and choose.

Charlie: Hey! You're helping / (breaking) that tree, Mary, and I love trees!
Mary: Yes, so do I. Sorry. You're right.
Charlie: Let's play soccer over there in the library / playground.
Mary: No, we can't. Those toys are for small children / pets.
Charlie: Oh, yes. Do you want to play soccer / badminton?
Mary: Yes, but we can't play next to the market / flowers. Let's go there.
Charlie: Yes, that's a great place to play soccer / buy food.

**2**  Listen and check.

**3** Put the words in order.

1 | at school. | It isn't OK | on the desks | to write |

---

2 | On the bus, | the floor. | feet on | put your |

---

3 | flowers in | Don't break the | the park. | trees and |

---

4 | throw your | You must not | the ground. | trash on |

---

**1**  Listen and number. CD3

**2** Complete. Choose the right answer.

want   win   help   hurts

1 You _____ . Good job!
   a) Yes, I'm a great player.
   b) Thank you. You're good at tennis, too.

2 Ow! My arm _____ .
   a) Do you want to play badminton?
   b) Can I help you? Should I get the teacher?

3 I don't _____ to play. I'm not very good at soccer.
   a) That's OK, John. We can help you.
   b) OK. Sit down and read a book.

4 Should I _____ you?
   a) Yes, please. Thanks very much!
   b) No, I don't want your help.

**1** Read and match.

1 Use public transportation.
2 Turn the water off when you wash your hair.
3 Take your bags with you when you go shopping.
4 Walk to school.
5 Turn the television off when you aren't watching it.
6 Don't use a lot of water when you wash your hands.

**2** Read and complete.

~~helping~~  take  bags  walks  always  water

Paul and Mary like (1) helping the world. Paul lives close to his school, so he (2) _____ there every day. Mary and her mom always (3) _____ the bus to stores, and they take their (4) _____ from home. Paul and Mary (5) _____ turn off the television when they aren't watching it. They don't use a lot of (6) _____ when they wash their hands and brush their teeth.

# Grammar reference

**1** Match the sentences.

1 What's Sally doing?          a) Yes, he is.
2 What are you doing?          b) He's kicking a ball.
3 What's Scott doing?          c) She's riding her bike.
4 Is Robert eating?           d) I'm reading a book.

**2** Look and circle the best answer.

1 Ben **likes** / **like** reading books.
2 Anna doesn't **enjoy** / **enjoys** taking a bath.
3 Grandma **want** / **wants** to ride her bike.
4 Mom doesn't **want** / **want to** give the dog a bath.

**3** Look and complete.      has   it has   Does   doesn't

Tom:   (1) _____ your new house have a balcony?

Vicky:  No, it (2) _____ have a balcony, but it

       (3) _____ a basement.

Tom:   Does it have a yard?

Vicky:  Yes, (4) _____ a big yard for my beautiful plants!

**4** Match the sentences.

1 What do you do before dinner?          a) Every day.
2 What time does Peter get dressed?       b) He sometimes plays in the park.
3 How often do you have homework?         c) He gets dressed at 8 o'clock.
4 What does Jim do after school?          d) I always wash my hands.

## 5 Read and order the words. Make sentences.

1  (buy food?)  (do you)  (go to)  (Where)

2  (you go)  (to)  (Where do)  (fly a kite?)

3  (you go to)  (Where)  (see a)  (doctor?)  (do)

1  _____

2  _____

3  _____

## 6 Look and complete.

(must not   Can   must   Must)

1  _____ I clean my shoes, Mom? Yes, you must.

2  You _____ listen to the teacher.

3  _____ I run in the playground? Yes, you can!

4  We _____ play tennis in the library.

## 7 Match the sentences.

1  I'm cold.          a) Should I get you a drink?

2  I'm hungry.        b) Should I get you a blanket?

3  I'm thirsty.       c) Should I make dinner?

## 8 Complete the sentences.

1  Horses are _____ than cows. (quick)

2  Sharks are _____ than whales. (small)

3  Bats are _____ than parrots. (dirty)

4  Dolphins are _____ at swimming than whales. (good)

## 9 Read and complete the sentences.

(wasn't   was   were   weren't)

On Saturday I (1) _____ at the beach with my family.

It (2) _____ hot and sunny, it was cold and windy!

There (3) _____ many children on the beach.

Where (4) _____ you on Saturday?

# About me

My birthday: ⸺⸺⸺⸺⸺⸺⸺⸺⸺⸺⸺⸺⸺⸺⸺⸺

Where I live: ⸺⸺⸺⸺⸺⸺⸺⸺⸺⸺⸺⸺⸺⸺⸺⸺

The language(s) I speak at home: ⸺⸺⸺⸺⸺⸺⸺⸺⸺⸺⸺

The language(s) I'm learning: ⸺⸺⸺⸺⸺⸺⸺⸺⸺⸺⸺

Write some sentences in the languages you know here.

Language: ⸺⸺⸺⸺⸺⸺⸺⸺⸺

⸺⸺⸺⸺⸺⸺⸺⸺⸺⸺⸺⸺⸺⸺⸺⸺
⸺⸺⸺⸺⸺⸺⸺⸺⸺⸺⸺⸺⸺⸺⸺⸺

Language: ⸺⸺⸺⸺⸺⸺⸺⸺⸺

⸺⸺⸺⸺⸺⸺⸺⸺⸺⸺⸺⸺⸺⸺⸺⸺
⸺⸺⸺⸺⸺⸺⸺⸺⸺⸺⸺⸺⸺⸺⸺⸺

Language: ⸺⸺⸺⸺⸺⸺⸺⸺⸺

⸺⸺⸺⸺⸺⸺⸺⸺⸺⸺⸺⸺⸺⸺⸺⸺
⸺⸺⸺⸺⸺⸺⸺⸺⸺⸺⸺⸺⸺⸺⸺⸺

# My language skills

| reading | writing | speaking | listening |
|---------|---------|----------|-----------|

**1** Write the word in the spaces below.

**2** Do you like doing these things in English? Color the faces.
Yellow = It's fantastic. Blue = It's good. Green = It's OK.

# I can ...　　　　Units 1-2

1 　 Listen. What's Sally doing? Check the boxes.

2 　 Say. This is Suzy's family. Who are they?

3 　 Read about the Star family's house. What do you think? Yes (✓) or no (✗)?

a　The Stars live in a small house. ☐

b　There's an upstairs and downstairs. ☐

c　They have a big yard. ☐

d　The bedrooms are downstairs. ☐

e　They don't have an elevator. ☐

4 　 Write about your home.

--------------------------------

--------------------------------

| Color the faces: I can do it! |
| :---: |
| 1  |
| 2  |
| 3  |
| 4 |

# I can ...                    # Units 3-4

Color
the faces:
I can do it!

**1** Listen and draw. What time is it?

a

b
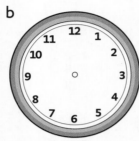

c

d

e

f

1

**2** Talk about your school day.

> I wake up at 7 o'clock. I eat breakfast at …

2

**3** Read and write the place.

a   You can fly a kite here. _____
b   You can buy CDs here. _____
c   You can get some money here. _____
d   You go here to catch a bus. _____
e   You can eat lunch or dinner here. _____
f   You go here to find a book. _____
g   You go here to swim. _____

3

**4** Write about your favorite store. What's its name? What can you buy there?

_____
_____
_____

4

# I can ...

# Units 5-6

**1**  Listen and point.

**2**  Say. What's good for you?

I go to sleep at ...
I wake up at ...
I play ...
I like eating ...

**3**  Read and draw.

In the middle of the picture there's a river. There's a field in front of the river and a forest behind it. Two people are having a picnic in the field. A boy's swimming in the river. There are flowers in the field.

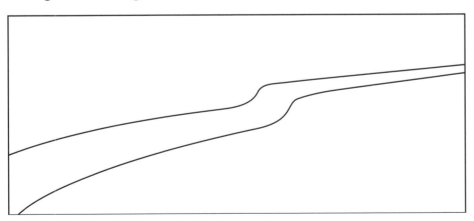

**4**  Write about you. Use four adjectives.

I'm _____

_____

_____

| 1 | 2 | 3 | 4 |

# I can ...

## Units 7-8

**1**  Listen to the descriptions and point to the animal.

**2** Say. Look at the pictures of the animals above. Describe them to your partner. Take turns.

> This animal is very big. It's bigger than a bat. It lives in the ...

**3** Read and draw.

It's cold today. It's raining and very windy. I'm wearing a hat and a scarf. I'm not happy. I want to go home and drink hot chocolate!

**4** Write. What do you wear?

When it's hot, I wear _____

When it's cold, _____

Now I'm wearing _____

Color the faces: I can do it!

1

2

3

4

# Learning English

1  I listen to English songs:

| a lot | sometimes | never |
|-------|-----------|-------|
|       |           |       |

2  I read books in English:

| a lot | sometimes | never |
|-------|-----------|-------|
|       |           |       |

3  I watch movies in English:

| a lot | sometimes | never |
|-------|-----------|-------|
|       |           |       |

How are you?

4  I speak to people in English:

| a lot | sometimes | never |
|-------|-----------|-------|
|       |           |       |

5  I have been to these places:

_____     _____

_____     _____

_____     _____

6  I spoke to people in English there:

| a lot | sometimes | never |
|-------|-----------|-------|
|       |           |       |

# My family

Draw or stick a picture of your family doing something you like to do together.

Who's in your picture? ------------------------------------------------------
------------------------------------------------------------------------------

What are you doing? ---------------------------------------------------------
------------------------------------------------------------------------------
------------------------------------------------------------------------------

# My home

Draw or stick a picture of your house or apartment.

My home is in:

the city ☐     a town ☐     the country ☐

My favorite room is ----------------------------------------- because I can

-----------------------------------------------------------------------

My house has -----------------------------------------------------------

-----------------------------------------------------------------------

# My school day

What do you do in the morning, the afternoon, and the evening on the days you go to school? Draw pictures and write sentences.

1  I wake up at
_____

2  _____
_____

3  _____
_____

4  _____
_____

5  _____
_____

6  _____
_____

My favorite day of the week is _____

because _____

_____

# Being healthy

Draw or stick a picture of you doing something healthy.

Circle "yes" or "no." Answer the questions.

1   I drink water: yes / no. How many glasses? _____

2   I eat fruit and vegetables: yes / no. What's your favorite fruit? _____
_____ . What's your favorite vegetable? _____ .

3   I exercise: yes / no. What sports do you like? _____ .

4   I like sleeping: yes / no. How many hours do you sleep? _____

# Outside

Draw or stick a picture of you outside in your favorite place. Is it a park? Is it the beach or the mountains? Is there a river, the ocean, or a lake? What animals can you see?

Where are you? ----------------------------------------------------------------

What can you do here? ----------------------------------------------------------

What can you see here? ---------------------------------------------------------

----------------------------------------------------------------------------------

----------------------------------------------------------------------------------

# A weather report

Look outside. What can you see? Draw your picture.
Add a thermometer. Is it cold or hot today?

What's the weather like today? _____

_____

My favorite weather is _____

_____